THE DARK TOWER

An Allegory — a story on two levels
- narrative level   Allos = other
- symbolic level.   Agoreuein = to speak.

A description of one thing under the guise of another which are suggestively similar. ie

by the same author

★

COLLECTED POEMS
SELECTED POEMS

THE
DARK TOWER

by

LOUIS MACNEICE

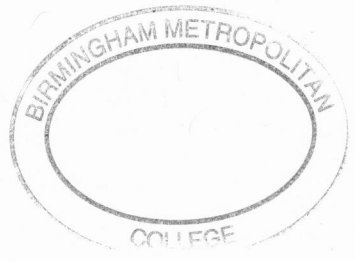

FABER AND FABER

London · Boston

First published in 1947
by Faber and Faber Limited
3 Queen Square London WC1
First published in this edition 1964
Reprinted 1967 and 1979
Printed in Great Britain by
Whitstable Litho Ltd., Whitstable, Kent.
All rights reserved

ISBN 0 571 06042 0

CONTENTS

Publishers' Note

This General Introduction was written by Louis MacNeice for *The Dark Tower : and Other Radio Scripts* which was published in 1947. Though the present edition contains *The Dark Tower* only, we decided to reprint the introduction as it was originally written.

GENERAL INTRODUCTION

THE interest shown in such few radio scripts as have been published (the most notable recent example being *The Rescue* by my friend Mr. Edward Sackville-West) has encouraged me to publish some more of my own. I do this not only because like all radio writers I feel frustrated each time a script has been broadcast but in the hope that a selection of dissimilar pieces may throw some light on the medium. I have chosen *The Dark Tower* because I think it the best radio script I have written; the others are included as fairly clear-cut examples—I would certainly not say models—of different types of programme. All of them seem to me worth reading.

Having in my Introduction to *Christopher Columbus* essayed a general exposition of radio-dramatic writing, I will not labour again those main points which I still consider valid, e.g. that 'the first virtue of a radio script is construction'. But I would like in some respects to correct myself. That the radio writer 'must move on a more or less primitive plane' is, I think now, an overstatement or at least misleadingly expressed. What the radio writer must do, if he hopes to win the freedom of the air, is to appeal *on one plane*—whatever he may be doing on the others—to the more primitive listener and to the more primitive elements in anyone; i.e. he must give them (what Shakespeare gave them) entertainment.[1]

In the same Introduction I wrote: 'As compared with most contemporary literature, the objective elements will preponderate over the subjective, statement over allusion, synthesis over analysis.' This again I want to qualify; the comparison with contemporary *literature* may have misled me. The 'psychological' novel, concerned chiefly with 'subjective' experiences, deals

[1] The reception of *The Dark Tower* supports this. Many listeners said that they enjoyed it, found it 'beautiful', 'exciting' etc.—but had 'no idea what it was about.' In fact they were caught by the 'story' but I flatter myself that, in passing, the story 'slipped over' some meaning on them.

9

largely in *oratio obliqua*; even that kind of *oratio recta* used to represent 'the stream of consciousness' is usually not much more than a shorthand for the page. But when no character can be presented except through spoken words, whether in dialogue or soliloquy, that very *spokenness* makes this distinction between subjective and objective futile. A character in a radio play, as in a stage play, may say things that actually he never would or could say—the author may be making him utter what is only known to his unconscious—but once he has said them, there they are! As objective as Ben Jonson's Humours are objective. To take an extreme example, Virginia Woolf's novel *The Waves* is often quoted as subjective writing *par excellence*; the characters, thinking in the first person, say things they never could have formulated, being even as small children endowed with the brilliant introspection and the sad philosophy of their creator. I am confident that this method, though probably not this application of it, would be feasible on the air. Listeners might not accept Virginia Woolf's long-windedness, her preciousness, the sameness of her characters, the lack of a 'story'—but that in no way proves them 'allergic' to subjectivity. Once your characters speak speakable lines—once, to use a horrible piece of jargon, the subjective is objectified—you can get away with anything *so long as you entertain*.

Similarly, the distinctions made in my quotation between statement and allusion and between synthesis and analysis are perhaps equally worthless. It would have been safer to say that in radio dialogue we need a number of things which *sound like* statements—but in spoken dialogue that goes without saying; no two people can keep up a conversation which is one *hundred* per cent surrealist. As for allusion, not only is it difficult in any context to make any statement which is not also an allusion, i.e. suggestive of something beyond its own definitive meaning, but in all *dramatic* writing a word, let alone a phrase, pulls more than its dictionary weight; the pun is only the crudest example of a pro-

General Introduction

cedure familiar to, though not of course formulated by, every-one. In characterisation equally, Mr. X, who may appear to be talking at random and naturalistically, can really be talking succinctly and also symbolically, revealing himself—or whatever else is meant to be revealed—by a process of implicit logic. 'Implicit' is here, as in other creative writing, a key-word. Even in the psychological novel, if it is a good one, the psychology is implicit; for explicit psychology we go to the textbooks. This is all I meant in subordinating analysis to synthesis—but this too could have gone without saying or at least I ought so to have expressed it as not to preclude 'psychological' characterisation from the sphere of radio drama.

But criticism comes after the event; it is no good talking about radio until you have experienced it. It may therefore be instruc-tive if, dropping generalities, I make a short confession of my own experiences as listener, script-writer, and producer. Before I joined the B.B.C. I was, like most of the intelligentsia, prejudiced not only against that institution but against broadcasting in general; I rarely listened to anything except concerts and running commentaries on sports events. These latter, which gave me a pleasure distinct from that which lies in *seeing* a game or race, should have provided a hint of radio's possibilities; my prejudice, however, prevented me from exploring the possible pleasures in wireless plays and features. Since then I have listened to many examples of both and must confess that often they give me no pleasure at all—but this proves nothing; we have all met the same disappointment with books, plays, and films. What does prove a point to me is that *some* plays and features have excited, amused, moved me. So the wireless *can* be worth listening to. But next: is it worth writing for?

Many writers are deterred from radio drama by fear of the middlemen and by dislike of actors. They expect their work to be doctored from the start and travestied in the presentation (which has of course sometimes happened—as it has happened both on the stage and page). But while no production will ever seem perfect to the author, the questions are whether one can gamble on a reasonably good production and whether such a production is better than none. Your answers depend on whether you really have an itch for drama; if you have, you must want sooner or later to write dialogue to be spoken somewhere—and it is no more likely to be spoken badly on the air than anywhere else (the wireless lacks the body of the stage—but also some of its impurities). If *you* provide a good script, the odds are that it will gain by being broadcast; in fact, if it loses, while it may be the fault of the production, the more likely inference is that your script was not radiogenic (a handy word, though jargon). The predominance of adapted stage-plays in B.B.C. programmes has probably discouraged a number of writers, for many of these plays do lose on the air (at least as compared with the stage); few of them are radiogenic. Transposition from one medium to another is usually unfair to both. Which is why we must remember that the script-writer is a peculiar species.

The all-important difference between visual and non-visual drama, while discouraging some, may encourage others towards radio, for here and here alone can one listen to calculated speech divorced from all visual supports or interferences—even from a printed page. It would be a great pity if television were ever completely to supersede sound broadcasting as the talkies superseded the silent films. That cinema revolution was inevitable but through it we lost the unique pleasure of watching a story told visually, dispensing with people's voices. But sound alone is for most people more potent, more pregnant, more subtle, than pictures alone and for that reason—regardless of the material pros and cons of television—I hope that sound broadcasting will survive, dispensing with people's faces. As with many other media its narrow limits are also its virtue, while within those limits it can give us something unobtainable from print (though print of course will always retain its proper autonomy). When I first

General Introduction

heard a piece, which I had written for broadcasting, broadcast, I was irritated by details of presentation but excited and delighted by the total effect (there was more to my script, I felt, than I myself had realised). The mere fact that one's words issue from other people's mouths, while gratifying no doubt to an author's vanity, is also a welcome release from his involuntary egotism. Most novelists and poets, I think, envy the playwright that specious present and that feeling of *sharedness* which are given to a play by every fresh production, just as they envy the painter as composer-executant the excitement of his manual craftsmanship and the immediate impact of his completed work (which also can be shared by several people at once). When you have written for the page, you do not see your readers reading you; which is just as well as you could never tell if in their heads they were 'hearing' you properly. But in broadcasting you can, given the right speakers, force your listeners at least to hear the words as they should. The point is that here we have a means by which written lines can emulate the impact of a stage or of a painting and give the writer that excitement of a sensuous experience simultaneously shared with many which is one of the joys of life. This pleasure in a thing-being-performed-and-shared, while obtainable in all sports and some of the arts, is sadly lacking in the world of literature today. It is a pleasure I have often received, though mixed at times with mortification, when hearing my own scripts broadcast. It is succeeded, as I said before, by a feeling of frustration—because it is 'over'; but in that it is not of course unusual.

I have stressed this fact of pleasure because some people assume that writing for the wireless must be hackwork. It often is—for the salaried script-writer because he must turn his hand to many things, some of them dull, for the occasional writer (less forgivably) when he deals with an uncongenial subject for money or writes badly because he is merely writing for money. But it often is not. Broadcasting is plastic; while it can ape the Press, it can

13

also emulate the arts. Yes, people will say, that is theoretically true but in practice you will never get art—or anything like it— out of a large public institution, encumbered with administrators, which by its nature must play for safety and to the gallery. This is not the place to dispute this at length but I would maintain that in this country such an institution cannot be really authoritarian; with ingenuity and a little luck a creative person can persuade (or fool) at least some of the administrators some of the time.[1] And, thinking of the vexed question of commercial broadcasting, I would add that many of the more original programmes by my friends and myself (this book shows examples in *The Dark Tower* and the 'March Hare' scripts) would have been no more acceptable to sponsored radio than to the biggest and vulgarest profit-making film company. For its acceptance of such experiments I am very grateful to the B.B.C.

In this age of irreconcilable idioms I have often heard writers hankering for some sort of group life, a desire doomed to disappointment; the modern writer—at any rate the modern poet— is *ipso facto* a spiritual isolationist who will lose far more than he will gain by trying to pool his mentality with those of his colleagues. Thus of the several dozen poets whom I know there are very few with whom I would wish to discuss poetry and only, I think, one from whom I would often accept criticism. This solitude (which incidentally has nothing to do with the Ivory Tower; there are Group Towers too, remember) is *in our time* salutary—but here again we cannot but envy playwrights, actors or musical executants. And here again I for one have found this missing group experience, in a valid form, in radio. Radio writers and producers *can* talk shop together because their shop is not, as with poets, a complex of spiritual intimacies but a matter of craftsmanship. Though the poet of course is also—or should be—a craftsman, the lyrical poet's technique is—or

[1] I am not suggesting that, as things are, all our administrators need persuading or fooling.

should be—closely wedded to his unique personality and there is no more point in defending your own personality than in impugning your friend's. But radio craftsmanship, like stage craftsmanship, is something much less private; we are fully entitled to discuss whether dialogue rings true, whether the dramatic climax is dramatic, how well the whole thing works. This is refreshing for a writer.

The popular assumption that all radio professionals resemble civil servants (resting on that other assumption that civil servants are automata) is flatly untrue. The department to which, at the date of writing, I belong in the B.B.C., would compare very well for intelligence with almost any contemporary salon of literati; my radio colleagues would be found on the whole quicker-witted, more versatile, less egocentric, less conventional, more humane. But, apart from these relishes to discussion, the reason why we can work together enjoyably and effectively is that in every case our work must go through the same mill, i.e. into a microphone and out at the other end through a wireless set. This very simple physical fact is such a bond of union as is rare among creative writers, playwrights again excepted. For we share the excitements and anxieties of *the performance*. This is especially so if we are our own executants, i.e. writer-producers. There are obvious drawbacks to this combination of functions—Mr. A as writer may see so clearly what he means that Mr. A as producer will fail to notice when the meaning is not coming over—but it does put a writer more closely in touch with his work-in-performance than he can be anywhere else unless he is Mr. Noel Coward. We know what happens to a film script when the multitude of 'experts' gets hold of it. On the stage there is no such multitude but there still is considerable interference and few writers have the chance, the time, the knowledge, or the capacity, to become stage-producers. But radio production being comparatively simple, not a few writers can learn to handle it—at any rate well enough to gain more than they lose (this especially applies to 'experimental' scripts where the pioneer, though an amateur, has an advantage over the professional geographer).

The script itself, after all, is only half the battle and the writer who merely sends in a script and does not go near the studios is working largely in the dark; whereas a writer who produces his own scripts will cut his coat according to his cloth. Since I have been producing my own programmes, I find that I both avail myself of facilities which I previously overlooked and avoid awkwardnesses which I previously imposed on my producer. Thus an earlier version of *Sunbeams in his Hat*, entitled *Dr. Chekhov*, was so written as to be almost unproduceable in places[1] at least without the use of multiple studios, as I typically had not envisaged the studio set-up. When I came to rewrite it for my own production I eliminated these difficulties and in so doing found I had made the script not only more manageable but more compact, more lucid, more convincing. Similarly, as regards both music and actors, the writer-producer has the advantage of being able to decide at an early stage who is going to do what. Thus, when he has a composer to write special music, he can not only get this music to fit the script but adjust his script on occasion to fit the music. He also has the say in casting, which is especially important in broadcasting both because of the shortness of rehearsals and because of the microphone's transparency to anything ham or unintelligent. In writing my more recent scripts I have always had an eye on the kinds of actor available and so avoided demanding the impossible and, when I could, the improbable; sometimes I have, from its conception, written a part for a particular actor, e.g. the Soldier in *The Nosebag* for Roy Emerton and the March Hare for Esmé Percy.

The preceding paragraph was intended to amplify my point about work-in-performance. While it is obviously not normally feasible for 'outside writers' to produce their own work, it is

[1] For which I now apologise to Mr. Stephen Potter—who in producing it saved the situation.

General Introduction

desirable, if not necessary, that they should be studio-minded; then they can explain to their producer what they want done without being embarrassing or nonsensical. I would like finally, since the chief object of this introduction was to disprove the assumption that broadcasting is 'inhuman', to inform my readers that every transmission of a play or feature, however unimportant the programme, should have—and usually has—the feeling of a First Night; it is something *being made* by a team of people.

For each of the scripts in this book I have written a separate introduction; but they all have this in common that, whatever my sins in either respect, I enjoyed both writing and producing them. The programme on Tchehov was suggested to me by my employers but the others I proposed myself. This gives me the opportunity of expressing my gratitude to the head of my department, Mr. Laurence Gilliam, who is as willing to accept such spontaneous suggestions as he is to allow an elastic treatment of those other programmes which 'have to be done'.

NOTES

The dialogue in these scripts is as broadcast but the directions have been re-written and considerably amplified.

The foregoing Introduction was written before the B.B.C. 'Third Programme' came into being. This new programme—for the first time, I believe, in radio history—assumes that its audience is going to *work* at its listening. So there is less question than ever of playing 'for safety and to the gallery'.

THE DARK TOWER

a radio parable play

TO

BENJAMIN BRITTEN

He also refers to the play as a
"cloved allegory." 1946.
"PRE CONCEPTIONS WAR"
It is realistic on the surface.
It is the symbolic core which makes
the work important.
Man does after all live by symbols.
Is there a clear moral or message

CAST

    The Dark Tower was first broadcast in the B.B.C. Home Service on January 21st, 1946. The main parts, in order of their appearance, were played as follows:

SERGEANT-TRUMPETER	HARRY HUTCHINSON*
GAVIN	FRANK PARTINGTON*
ROLAND	CYRIL CUSACK
MOTHER	OLGA LINDO
TUTOR	MARK DIGNAM
SYLVIE	LUCILLE LISLE*
BLIND PETER	IVOR BARNARD
SOAK	ROBERT FARQUHARSON
STEWARD	HOWARD MARION-CRAWFORD
NEAERA	VERA MAXIME
SHIP'S OFFICER	CHARLES MAUNSELL*
PRIEST	ALEXANDER SARNER*
ROLAND'S FATHER	LAIDMAN BROWNE*
PARROT	MARJORIE WESTBURY*
RAVEN	STANLEY GROOME*
CLOCK VOICE	DUNCAN MCINTYRE*

Special music was composed by Benjamin Britten and conducted by Walter Goehr.

The production was by the author.

   * A star denotes membership of the B.B.C. Repertory Company at the time of the broadcast. It will be seen from this and the other lists of cast in the book how useful this institution is.

INTRODUCTORY NOTE

The Dark Tower is a parable play, belonging to that wide class of writings which includes *Everyman*, *The Faerie Queene* and *The Pilgrim's Progress*. Though under the name of allegory this kind of writing is sometimes dismissed as outmoded, the clothed as distinct from the naked allegory is in fact very much alive. Obvious examples are *Peer Gynt* and the stories of Kafka but also in such books as *The Magic Mountain* by Thomas Mann, where the disguise of 'realism' is maintained and nothing happens that is quite inconceivable in life, it is still the symbolic core which makes the work important. My own impression is that pure 'realism' is in our time almost played out, though most works of fiction of course will remain realistic *on the surface*. The single-track mind and the single-plane novel or play are almost bound to falsify the world in which we live. The fact that there is method in madness and the fact that there is fact in fantasy (and equally fantasy in 'fact') have been brought home to us not only by Freud and other psychologists but by events themselves. This being so, reportage can no longer masquerade as art. So the novelist, abandoning the 'straight' method of photography, is likely to resort once more not only to the twist of plot but to all kinds of other twists which may help him to do justice to the world's complexity. Some element of parable therefore, far from making a work thinner and more abstract, ought to make it more concrete. Man does after all live by symbols.

The dual-plane work will not normally be allegory in the algebraic sense; i.e. it will not be desirable or even possible to equate each of the outward and visible signs with a precise or rational inner meaning. Thus *The Dark Tower* was suggested to me by Browning's poem 'Childe Roland to the Dark Tower came', a work which does not admit of a completely rational analysis and still less adds up to any clear moral or message. This poem has the solidity of a dream; the writer of such a poem, though he may be

The Dark Tower

aware of the 'meanings' implicit in his dream, must not take the dream to pieces, must present his characters concretely, must allow the story to persist as a story and not dwindle into a diagram. While I could therefore have offered here an explicit summary of those implicit 'meanings' in *The Dark Tower* of which I myself was conscious, I am not doing so, because it might impair the impact of the play. I would merely say—for the benefit of people like the *Daily Worker's* radio critic, who found the programme pointless and depressing—that in my opinion it is neither. *The Faerie Queene*, *The Pilgrim's Progress*, *Piers Plowman* and the early Moralities could not have been written by men without any beliefs. In an age which precludes the simple and militant faith of a Bunyan, belief (whether consciously formulated or not) still remains a *sine qua non* of the creative writer. I have my beliefs and they permeate *The Dark Tower*. But do not ask me what Ism it illustrates or what Solution it offers. You do not normally ask for such things in the single-plane work; why should they be forced upon something much more complex? 'Why, look you now, how unworthy a thing you make of me!' What is life *useful* for anyway?

Comments on points of detail will be found at the end of this book. The best in this kind are but shadows—and in print they are shadows of shadows. To help the reader to *hear* this piece, I will therefore add this: in production I got the actors to play their parts 'straight', i.e. like flesh and blood (in dreams the characters are usually like flesh and blood too). Out of an excellent cast I am particularly grateful to Cyril Cusack for his most sensitive rendering of 'Roland'. And Benjamin Britten provided this programme with music which is, I think, the best I have heard in a radio play. Without his music *The Dark Tower* lacks a dimension.

THE DARK TOWER

OPENING ANNOUNCEMENT

*The Dark Tower. The programme which follows is a parable play—
suggested by Robert Browning's poem 'Childe Roland to the Dark Tower
came'. The theme is the ancient but ever-green theme of the Quest—the
dedicated adventure; the manner of presentation is that of a dream—but
a dream that is full of meaning. Browning's poem ends with a challenge
blown on a trumpet:*

> 'And yet
> *Dauntless the slughorn to my lips I set*
> *And blew. ''Childe Roland to the Dark Tower came''.'*

*Note well the words 'And yet'. Roland did not have to—he did not wish
to—and yet in the end he came to: The Dark Tower.*

(*A trumpet plays through the Challenge Call.*)

SERGEANT-TRUMPETER.

There now, that's the challenge. And mark this:
Always hold the note at the end.

GAVIN. Yes, Sergeant-Trumpeter, yes.

ROLAND (*as a boy*).

Why need Gavin hold the note at the end?

SERGEANT-TRUMPETER.

Ach, ye're too young to know. It's all tradition.

ROLAND. What's tradition, Sergeant-Trumpeter?

GAVIN. Ask Mother that one (*with a half-laugh*). She knows.

SERGEANT-TRUMPETER.

Aye, *she* knows.
But run along, sonny. Leave your brother to practise.
(*The trumpet begins—but breaks off.*)

SERGEANT-TRUMPETER.

No. Again.
(*The trumpet re-begins—breaks off.*)

23

SERGEANT-TRUMPETER.

> Again.

> > (*The trumpet re-begins and is sustained.*)

SERGEANT-TRUMPETER.

> That's it now. But hold that last note—hold it!

> (*On the long last note the trumpet fades into the distance.*)

ROLAND. Mother! What's tradition?

MOTHER. Hand me that album. No—the black one.

ROLAND. Not the locked one!

MOTHER. Yes, the locked one. I have the key.

> Now, Roland, sit here by me on the sofa.

> We'll look at them backwards.

ROLAND. Why must we look at them backwards?

MOTHER. Because then you may recognise—

> Now! You know who this is?

ROLAND. Why, that's my brother Michael.

> And here's my brother Henry!

> Michael and Henry and Denis and Roger and John!

> (*He speaks with the bright callousness of children.*)

> Do you keep this album locked because they're dead?

MOTHER. No . . . not exactly.

> Now—can you guess who this is?

ROLAND. That's someone I saw in a dream once.

MOTHER. It must have been in a dream.

> He left this house three months before you were born.

ROLAND. Is it . . . is it my father?

MOTHER. Yes. And this is your grandfather. And this is *his* father—

> For the time being you needn't look at the rest;

> This book goes back through seven long generations

> As far as George the founder of the family.

ROLAND. And did they all die the same way?

MOTHER. They did, Roland. And now I've answered your question.

The Dark Tower

ROLAND (*already forgetting*).

    What question, Mother?

    (*The trumpet call is heard in the distance.*)

ROLAND. Ah, there's Gavin practising.

    He's got it right at last.

    (*The Call ends and Gavin appears.*)

GAVIN (*excited*).

    Mother! I know the challenge. When can I leave?
    Tomorrow?

MOTHER. Why not today, Gavin?

GAVIN. Today! But I haven't yet checked my equipment;
    I mean——for such a long journey I—

MOTHER. You will travel light, my son.

GAVIN. Well, yes . . . of course . . . today then.

ROLAND. Where are you going, Gavin?

GAVIN. Why, surely you know; I'm—

MOTHER. Hsh!

ROLAND. I know where he's going. Across the sea like Michael.

GAVIN. That's right, Roland. Across the big, bad sea.
    Like Michael and Henry and Denis and Roger and
    John.
    And after that through the Forest.
    And after that through the Desert—

ROLAND. What's the Desert made of?

GAVIN. Well . . . I've never been there.
    Some deserts are made of sand and some are made of
    grit but—

MOTHER (*as if to herself*).

    This one is made of doubts and dried-up hopes.

ROLAND (*still bright*).

    And what do you find at the other end of the desert?

GAVIN. Well, I . . . well . . .

MOTHER. You can tell him.

GAVIN. I find the Dark Tower.

The Dark Tower

(The Dark Tower theme gives a musical transition to the schoolroom.)

TUTOR. Now, Master Roland, as this is our first day of lessons
　　　　I trust I shall find you as willing a pupil
　　　　As your six brothers before you.

ROLAND. Did you like teaching my brothers?

TUTOR. Like it? It was an honour.
　　　　It was teaching to some purpose.

ROLAND. When's my brother Gavin coming back?

TUTOR. What!

ROLAND. Gavin. When's he coming back?

TUTOR. Roland! . . .
　　　　I see I must start from the beginning.
　　　　I thought your mother'd have told you but maybe
　　　　　being the youngest—

ROLAND. What would my mother have told me?

TUTOR. You ask when your brother Gavin is coming back?
　　　　You must get this straight from the start:
　　　　Your family never come back.
　　　　(Roland begins to interrupt.)

TUTOR. Now, now, now, don't let me scare you.
　　　　Sit down on that stool and I'll try to explain.
　　　　Now, Roland—
　　　　I said that to teach your brothers was an honour.
　　　　Before your mother engaged me to tutor John
　　　　I was an usher in a great city,
　　　　I taught two dozen lads in a class—
　　　　The sons of careerists—salesmen, middlemen, half-
　　　　　men,
　　　　Governed by greed and caution; it was my job
　　　　To teach them enough—and only enough—
　　　　To fit them for making money. Means to a means.
　　　　But with your family it is a means to an end.

ROLAND *(naïvely puzzled)*.
　　　　My family don't make money?

26

The Dark Tower

TUTOR. They make history.

ROLAND. And what do you mean by an end?

TUTOR. I mean—surely they told you?
I mean: the Dark Tower.

ROLAND. Will *I* ever go to the Dark Tower?

TUTOR. Of course you will. That is why I am here.

ROLAND (*gaily*).
Oh well! That's different!

TUTOR. It is.

ROLAND. And that means I'll fight the Dragon?

TUTOR. Yes—but let me tell you:
We call it the Dragon for short, it is a nameless force
Hard to define—for no one who has seen it,
Apart from those who have seen its handiwork,
Has returned to give an account of it.
All that we know is there is something there
Which makes the Dark Tower dark and is the source
Of evil through the world. It is immortal
But men must try to kill it—and keep on trying
So long as we would be human.

ROLAND. What would happen
If we just let it alone?

TUTOR. Well .... some of us would live longer; all of us
Would lead a degraded life, for the Dragon would be
supreme
Over our minds as well as our bodies. Gavin—
And Michael and Henry and Denis and Roger and
John—
Might still be here—perhaps your father too,
He would be seventy-five—but mark this well:
They would not be themselves. Do you understand?

ROLAND. I'm not quite sure, I . . .

TUTOR. You are still small. We'll talk of the Dragon later.
Now come to the blackboard and we'll try some Latin.

You see this sentence?

ROLAND. Per ardúa . . .

TUTOR. Per ardua ad astra.

ROLAND. What does it mean?

TUTOR. It does not go very well in a modern language.

We had a word 'honour'—but it is obsolete.

Try the word 'duty'; and there's another word—
'Necessity'.

ROLAND. Necessity! That's a bit hard to spell.

TUTOR. You'll have to spell it, I fear. Repeat this after me:
N—

ROLAND. N—

TUTOR. E—

ROLAND. E—

(*As they spell it through, their voices dwindle away and a tolling bell grows up out of the distance.*)

SERGEANT-TRUMPETER.

Ah God, there's the bell for Gavin.

He had the greatest power to his lungs of the lot of
them.

And now he's another name in the roll of honour

Where Michael's is still new gold. Five years it is—

Or would it be more like six—since we tolled for
Michael?

Bells and trumpets, trumpets and bells,

I'll have to be learning the young one next;

Then he'll be away too and my lady will have no more.

MOTHER (*coldly; she has come up behind him*).

No more children, Sergeant-Trumpeter?

SERGEANT-TRUMPETER.

Ach, I beg your pardon. I didn't see you.

MOTHER. No matter. But know this:

I have one more child to bear.

No, I'm not mad; you needn't stare at me, Sergeant.

This is a child of stone.

SERGEANT-TRUMPETER.

A child of . . . ?

MOTHER. Stone. To be born on my death-bed.

No matter. I'm speaking in metaphor.

SERGEANT-TRUMPETER (*relieved to change the subject*).

That's all right then. How's young Roland
Making out at his lessons?

MOTHER. I don't know. Roland lacks concentration; he's not
like my other sons,

He's almost flippant, he's always asking questions—

SERGEANT-TRUMPETER.

Ach, he's young yet.

MOTHER. Gavin was his age once.

So were Michael and Henry and Denis and Roger and
John.

They never forgot what they learnt. And they asked
no questions.

SERGEANT-TRUMPETER.

Ah well—by the time that Roland comes to me
When he's had his fill of theory and is all set for
action,

In another half dozen years when he comes to learn
the trumpet call—

MOTHER. Hsh, don't talk of it now.

(*as if to herself*).

Let one bell toll at a time.

(*The bell recedes into nothing, covering a passage of years. Roland is now
grown up.*)

TUTOR. So ends our course on ethics. Thank you, Roland;
After all these years our syllabus is concluded.
You have a brain; what remains to be tried is your will.
Remember our point today: the sensitive man
Is the more exposed to seduction. In six years

I have come to know you; you have a warm heart—
It is perhaps too warm for a man with your com-
    mission,
Therefore be careful. Keep to your one resolve,
Your single code of conduct, listen to no one
Who doubts your values—and above all, Roland,
Never fall in love—That is not for you.
If ever a hint of love should enter your heart,
You must arise and go . . . . That's it: Go!
Yes, Roland my son. Go quickly.

(His last words fade slightly and Sylvie's voice fades in.)

SYLVIE. But why must you go so quickly? Now that the sun's
        come out.

ROLAND. I have my lesson to learn.

SYLVIE. You're always learning lessons!
        I'll begin to think you prefer your books to me.

ROLAND. Oh, but Sylvie, this isn't books any more.

SYLVIE. Not books? Then—

ROLAND. I'm learning to play the trumpet.

SYLVIE (*irritated*).

        Whatever for? Roland, you make me laugh.
        Is this another idea of your mother's?
        I needn't ask. What's all this leading to?

ROLAND (*quietly*).

        I could tell you, darling. But not today.
        Today is a thing in itself—apart from the future.
        Whatever follows, I will remember this tree
        With this dazzle of sun and shadow—and I will
            remember
        The mayflies jigging above us in the delight
        Of the dying instant—and I'll remember *you*
        With the bronze lights in your hair.

SYLVIE. Yes, darling; but why so sad?
        There will be other trees and—

ROLAND. Each tree is itself, each moment is itself,
        Inviolable gifts of time . . . of God—
        But you cannot take them with you.

SYLVIE. Take them with you where?

ROLAND. Kiss me, Sylvie. I'm keeping my teacher waiting.
        (*The Challenge Call is played through once.*)

SERGEANT-TRUMPETER.
        Nicely blown! Nicely blown!
        You've graduated, my lad.
        But remember—when I'm not here—hold the note
          at the end.

ROLAND. (*a shade bitter*).
        You mean when *I'm* not here.

SERGEANT-TRUMPETER.
        Aye, you're right. But you are my last pupil,
        I'll be shutting up shop, I want you to do me credit.
        When you've crossed the sea and the desert and come
          to the place itself
        I want you to do me credit when you unsling that
          horn.

ROLAND. I hope I will.
        (*He pauses; then slightly embarrassed.*)

ROLAND. Sergeant?

SERGEANT-TRUMPETER.
        Eh?

ROLAND. Do you believe in all this?

SERGEANT-TRUMPETER.
        All what?

ROLAND. Do you think that there really is any dragon to fight?

SERGEANT-TRUMPETER.
        What are you saying! What was it killed Gavin?
        And Michael and Henry and Denis and Roger and John,
        And your father himself and his father before him and
          all of them back to George!

ROLAND. I don't know but . . . nobody's *seen* this dragon.

SERGEANT-TRUMPETER.

Seen him? They've seen what he's done!

Have you never talked to Blind Peter?

I thought not. Cooped up here in the castle—

Inside this big black ring of smothering yew-trees—

You never mixed with the folk.

But before you leave—if you want a reason for leaving—

I recommend that you pay a call on Peter.

And his house is low; mind your head as you enter.

(*Another verbal transition.*)

BLIND PETER (*old and broken*).

That's right, sir; mind your head as you enter.

Now take that chair, it's the only one with springs,

I saved it from my hey-day. Well now, sir,

It's kind of you to visit me. I can tell

By your voice alone that you're your father's son;

Your handshake's not so strong though.

ROLAND. Why, was my father—

BLIND PETER.

He had a grip of iron.

And what's more, sir, he had a will of iron.

And what's still more again, he had a conscience—

Which is something we all need. *I* should know!

ROLAND. Why?

BLIND PETER.

Why what?

ROLAND. Why do you sound so sad when you talk about having a conscience?

BLIND PETER.

Because his conscience is something a man can lose.

It's cold in here, I'll make a long story short.

Fifty years ago when I had my sight—

But the Dragon was loose at the time—
I had a job and a wife and a new-born child
And I believed in God. Until one day—
I told you the Dragon was loose at the time,
No one had challenged him lately; so he came out
    from his den—
What some people call the Tower—and creeping
    around
He got to our part of the world; nobody saw him of
    course,
There was just like a kind of a bad smell in the air
And everything went sour; people's mouths and eyes
Changed their look overnight—and the government
    changed too—
And as for me I woke up feeling different
And when I looked in the mirror that first morning
The mirror said 'Informer'!

ROLAND (*startled*).

    Informer?

BLIND PETER.

    Yes, sir. My new rôle.
    They passed a pack of laws forbidding this and that
    And anyone breaking 'em—the penalty was death.
    I grew quite rich sending men to their death.
    The last I sent was my wife's father.

ROLAND. But . . . but did you believe in these laws?

BLIND PETER.

    Believe? Aha! Did I believe in anything?
    God had gone round the corner. I was acquiring
      riches.
    But to make a long story short—
    When they hanged my wife's father my wife took
      poison,
    So I was left with the child. Then the child took ill—

        Scared me stiff—so I sent for all the doctors,

        I could afford 'em then—but they couldn't discover

        Anything wrong in its body, it was more as if its soul

        Was set on quitting—and indeed why not?

        To be a human being, people agree, is difficult.

ROLAND. Then the child . . . ?

BLIND PETER.

        Quit.

        Yes; she quit—but slowly.

        I watched it happen. That's why now I'm blind.

ROLAND. Why? You don't mean you yourself—

BLIND PETER.

        When you've seen certain things, you don't want to
           see no more.

        Tell me, sir. Are people's faces nowadays

        As ugly as they were? You know what I mean: evil?

ROLAND. No, not most of them. *Some*, I suppose—

BLIND PETER.

        Those ones belong to the Dragon.

ROLAND (*exasperated*).

        Why put the blame of everything on the Dragon?

        Men have free choice, haven't they?

        Free choice of good or evil—

BLIND PETER.

        That's just it—

        And the evil choice is the Dragon!

        But I needn't explain it to you, sir; *you've* made up
           your mind,

        You're like your father—one of the dedicated

        Whose life is a quest, whose death is a victory.

        Yes! God bless you! *You've* made up your mind!

ROLAND (*slowly and contemplatively*).

        But have I, Peter? Have I?

                (*Verbal transition.*)

SYLVIE. Have you, Roland dearest? Really made up your
mind?

ROLAND (*without expression*).

I go away today.

SYLVIE. That's no answer.

You go away because they tell you to.

Because your mother's brought you up on nothing

But out of date beliefs and mock heroics.

It's easy enough for her—

ROLAND (*indignantly*).

Easy for her?

Who's given her flesh and blood—and I'm the seventh
son!

SYLVIE. I've heard all that. They call it sacrifice

But each new death is a stone in a necklace to her.

Your mother, Roland, is mad.

ROLAND (*with quiet conviction*).

The world is mad.

SYLVIE. Not all of it, my love. Those who have power

Are mad enough but there *are* people, Roland,

Who keep themselves to themselves or rather to each
other,

Living a sane and gentle life in a forest nook or a hill
pocket,

Perpetuating their kind and their kindness, keeping

Their hands clean and their eyes keen, at one
with

Themselves, each other and nature. I had thought

That you and I perhaps—

ROLAND.   There is no perhaps

In my tradition, Sylvie.

SYLVIE. You mean in your family's.

Isn't it time you saw that you were different?

You're no knight errant, Roland.

ROLAND. No, I'm not.

But there is a word 'Necessity'—

SYLVIE. Necessity? You mean your mother's orders.

ROLAND (*controlled*).

Not quite. But apart from that,

I saw a man today—they call him Blind Peter—

SYLVIE. Leave the blind to mislead the blind. That Peter

Is where he is because of his own weakness;

You can't help him, Roland.

ROLAND. Maybe not—

(*with sudden insight*).

But maybe I can do something to prevent

A recurrence of Blind Peters.

SYLVIE. Imagination!

ROLAND. Imagination? . . . That things can be bettered?

That action can be worth-while? That there are ends

Which, even if not reached, are worth approaching?

Imagination? Yes, I wish I had it—

I have a little—You should support that little

And not support my doubts.

(*A drum-roll is heard.*)

ROLAND. Listen; there is the drum.

They are waiting for me at the gate.

Sylvie, I—

SYLVIE. Kiss me at least.

(*Pause, while the drum changes rhythm.*)

ROLAND. I shall never—

SYLVIE. See me again?

You will, Roland, you will.

I know you. You will set out but you won't go on,

Your common sense will triumph, you'll come back.

And your love for me will triumph and in the end—

ROLAND. This is the end. Goodbye.

(*The drum swells and ends on a peak. This is the Scene of Departure.*)

The Dark Tower

TUTOR. To you, Roland, my last message:

For seven years I have been your tutor.

You have worked hard on the whole but whether really

You have grasped the point of it all remains to be seen.

A man lives on a sliding staircase—

Sliding downwards, remember; to be a man

He has to climb against it, keeping level

Or even ascending slightly; he will not reach

The top—if there is a top—and when he dies

He will slump and go down regardless. All the same

While he lives he must climb. Remember that.

And I thank you for your attention. Goodbye, Roland.

SERGEANT-TRUMPETER.

To you, Roland, my last message:

You are off now on the Quest like your brothers before you

To take a slap at the Evil that never dies.

Well, here's this trumpet; sling it around your waist

And keep it bright and clean till the time comes

When you have to sound the challenge—the first and the last time—

And I trust you will do your old instructor credit

And put the fear of God—or of Man—into that Dragon.

That's all now. God bless you. But remember—

Hold that note at the end.

MOTHER. To you, Roland, my last message:

Here is a ring with a blood-red stone. So long as

This stone retains its colour, it means that I

Retain my purpose in sending you on the Quest.

I put it now on your finger.

ROLAND. Mother! It burns.

37

The Dark Tower

MOTHER. That is the heat in the stone. So long as the stone is red
The ring will burn and that small circle of fire
Around your little finger will be also
The circle of my will around your mind.
I gave a ring like this to your father, Roland,
And to John and Roger and Denis and Henry and Michael
And to Gavin the last before you. My will was around and behind them.
Should ever you doubt or waver, look at this ring—
And feel it burn—and go on.

ROLAND. Mother! Before I go—

MOTHER. No more words. Go!
Turn your face to the sea. (*Raising her voice.*) Open the gates there!
(*aside*) The March of Departure, Sergeant.
Let my son go out—my last. And make the music gay!

(*The March begins at full volume, then gradually dwindles as Roland and the listener move away. By the time the music has vanished Roland has reached the Port, where he addresses a stranger.*)

ROLAND. Forgive me stopping you, sir—

SOAK (*old, alcoholic, leering*).
Forgive you? Certainly not.
I'm on my way to the Tavern.

ROLAND. I'm on my way to the quays. Is it this turning or next?

SOAK. Any turning you like. Look down these stinking streets—
There's sea at the end of each of 'em.
Yes, young man, but what's at the end of the sea?
Never believe what they said when you booked your passage.

ROLAND. But I haven't booked it yet.

38

SOAK. Not booked your passage yet! Why, then there's no
        need to hurry.
        You come with me to the Tavern; it's only a step.

ROLAND. I cannot spare a step.

SOAK. All right, all right;
        If you won't come to the Tavern, the Tavern must
        come to you.
        Ho there, music!

(The orchestra strikes up raggedly—continuing while he speaks.)

SOAK. That's the idea. Music does wonders, young man.
        Music can build a palace, let alone a pub.
        Come on, you masons of the Muses, swing it,
        Fling me up four walls. Now, now, don't drop your
        tempo;
        Easy with those hods. All right; four walls.
        Now benches—tables—No! No doors or windows.
        What drunk wants daylight? But you've left out the bar.
        Come on—'Cellos! Percussion! All of you! A bar!
        That's right. Dismiss!

                    (The music ends.)

SOAK. Barmaid.

BARMAID. Yes, sir?

SOAK. Give us whatever you have and make it triple.

ROLAND. Just a small one for me, please.

SOAK. Oh don't be so objective. One would think,
        Looking at your long face, that there's a war on.

ROLAND. But—

SOAK. There is no war on—and you have no face.
        Drink up. Don't be objective.

ROLAND. What in the name of—

BARMAID. Look, dearie; don't mind *him*.
        He always talks like that. You take my tip;
        You're new here and this town is a sea-port,
        The tone is rather . . . . You go somewhere inland.

ROLAND. But how can I?

    I have to go to sea.

BARMAID (*seriously*).

    The sea out there leads nowhere.

SOAK. Come, sweetheart, the same again.

BARMAID. Nowhere, I've warned you. (*In a whisper.*) As for our
    friend here,

    Don't stay too long in his company.

SOAK. What's that? Don't stay too long in my what?

BARMAID. Company was the word.

SOAK. Company? I have none. Why, how could I?

    There's never anyone around where I am.

    I exist for myself and all the rest is projection.

    Come on, projection, drink! Dance on your strings
    and drink!

BARMAID. Oblige him, dearie, oblige him.

SOAK. There! My projection drinks.

    I wrote this farce before I was born, you know—

    This puppet play. In my mother's womb, dear boy—

    I have never abdicated the life of the womb.

    Watch, Mabel: my new puppet drinks again—

    A pretty boy but I've given him no more lines.

    Have I, young man?

                (*pause*)

    You see, he cannot speak.

    All he can do henceforward is to drink—

    Look! A pull on the wire—the elbow lifts.

    Give him the same again.

BARMAID. Well . . . .

SOAK. There is no well about it. Except the well

    That has no bottom and that fills the world.

    Triplets, I said. Where are those damned musicians?

    Buck up, you puppets! Play!

(*The orchestra strikes up a lullaby, continued behind his speech.*)

The Dark Tower

SOAK (*sleepily*).

> Good. Serenade me now till I fall asleep
> And all the notes are one—and all the sounds are
>   silence.
> Unity, Mabel, unity is my motto.
> The end of drink is a whole without any parts—
> A great black sponge of night that fills the world
> And when you squeeze it, Mabel, it drips inwards.
> D'you want me to squeeze it? Right. Piano there.
> Piano—I must sleep. Didn't you hear me?
> Piano, puppets. All right, pianissimo.
> Nissimo . . . nissimo . . . issimo . . . .
>
> (*The music ends and only his snoring is heard.*)

ROLAND. A puppet? . . . A projection? . . . How he lies!

> And yet I've sometimes thought the same, you
>   know—
> The same but the other way round.
> There is no evidence for anything
> Except my own existence—he says his.
> But he's wrong anyway—look at him snoring there.
> If I were something existing in his mind
> How could I go on now that he's asleep?

SOAK (*muffled*).

> Because I'm dreaming you.

ROLAND. Dreaming?

BARMAID. Yes, sir.

> He does have curious dreams.

SOAK. Yes, and the curious thing about my dreams

> Is that they always have an unhappy ending
> For all except the dreamer. Thus at the moment
> You'd never guess, young man, what rôle I've cast
>   you for—

ROLAND. What the—

BARMAID. Never mind, dear.

Tomorrow he'll wake up.

ROLAND. Tomorrow *he'll* wake up?

And I—Shall I wake up? Perhaps to find

That this whole Quest is a dream. Perhaps I'm still at home

In my bed by the window looking across the valley

Between the yew-trees to where Sylvie lives

Not among yews but apples—

(He is interrupted by a terrific voice crashing in on the 'Bar' from the outer world.)

STENTOR. All Aboard!

ROLAND. What's that?

STENTOR. All Aboard!

SOAK. You'd never guess

What happens in my dream . . . .

STENTOR. All Aboard! All Aboard!

Come along there, young man—unless you want to be left.

All Aboard for the Further Side of the Sea,

For the Dead End of the World and the Bourne of No Return!

(The noise of a crowd materialises, increasing.)

STENTOR. All Aboard, ladies and gents, knaves and fools, babes and sucklings,

Philistines, pharisees, parasites, pimps,

Nymphos and dipsos—All Aboard!

Lost souls and broken bodies; make it snappy.

That's right, folks. Mind your feet on the gangway.

(Through the racket of gadarening passengers is heard the mechanical voice of the Ticket Collector.)

TICKET COLLECTOR.

Ticket? Thank you . . . Ticket? Thank you . . .

Ticket? Thank you . . . Ticket? Thank you . . . .

(The crowd noises fade out; Roland is now below decks.)

The Dark Tower

STEWARD (*with an 'off-straight' accent*).

This way, sir. Let me show you your stateroom.

Hot and cold and a blue light over the bed.

Ring once for a drink, twice for an aspirin.

Now if you want anything else—a manicure, for example—

ROLAND. No, steward. A sleeping draught.

STEWARD (*archly*).

Sir! In the morning?

ROLAND. Morning be damned. My head aches.

STEWARD. Drinking last night, sir?

ROLAND. Thinking.

STEWARD (*rattling it off*).

Thinking? That's too bad, sir.

But you'll soon get over that, sir.

In this ship nobody thinks, sir.

Why should they? They're at sea, sir . . .

And if your brain's at sea, sir—

ROLAND (*angrily*).

Listen! I want a sleeping draught.

How many times do I have to ring for that?

STEWARD (*unperturbed*).

As many times as you like, sir.

If you can keep awake, sir.

(*pimpishly*) But talking of sleeping draughts, sir,

Do you hear that lady playing the fiddle?

ROLAND. Fiddle? No. I don't.

STEWARD. Ah, that's because she plays it in her head.

But she's a very nice lady, sir.

Her name, sir, is Neaera.

ROLAND. Why should I care what her name is?

I tell you, steward—

STEWARD. Of course if you'd rather play tombola—

ROLAND. Tombola?

STEWARD (*throwing it away*).

> Game of chance, sir. They call out numbers.
>
> Kills the time, sir. Rather like life, sir.
>
> You can buy your tickets now in the lounge.
>
> The ship's started, you know, sir.

ROLAND. Oh, so the ship's started?

(*worried*) But I can't hear the engines.

STEWARD. Can't you, sir? I was right then.

ROLAND. Right? What do you mean?

STEWARD. I thought so the moment I saw you.

> You don't, sir; of course you don't.

ROLAND. Don't what, damn you? Don't what?

STEWARD. *You* don't know where you're going, sir.

> (*The ship's engines are heard on the orchestra; from them emerges the chatter of the lounge with the banal laughter of tombola players.*)

OFFICER. Clickety-click; sixty-six . . .

> Kelly's Eye: Number One . . .
>
> And we—

CROWD (*raggedly*).

> Shake the Bag!
>
> (*The orchestral engines give place to a solo violin.*)

NEAERA (*to herself, velvety*).

> . . . Andantino . . . rallentando . . . adagio—
>
> (*Her violin-playing breaks off.*)

NEAERA (*foreign accent*).

> Mon Dieu! You startled me.

ROLAND. I'm sorry, I—

NEAERA (*cooingly*).

> Do sit down. So you're going Nowhere too?

ROLAND. On the contrary, Madam—

NEAERA. Call me Neaera.

ROLAND. But—

NEAERA. And I'll call you Roland.

ROLAND. How do you know my name?

NEAERA. A little bird told me. A swan, if you want to know;
He sang your name and he died.
That's right, sit down. I've seen your dossier too.

ROLAND. Seen my—

NEAERA. Oh yes, chéri. In the Captain's cabin.

ROLAND. But how can I have a dossier? I've done nothing.

NEAERA. That's just it. It's dull.
But the future part amuses me.
Oh yes, my dear, this dossier includes the future—
And you don't come out of it well.

ROLAND. What do you mean?

NEAERA. You never believed in this Quest of yours, you see—
The Dark Tower—the Dragon—all this blague.
That's why you were so easy to seduce
In the idle days at sea—the days that are just begin-
ning.

(*Her violin begins again, then gives way to the lounge chatter, covering a
passage of time.*)

OFFICER. Key of the Door: Twenty-One!
Eleventh Hour: Eleven!
Ten Commandments: Nine!
Kelly's Eye: Number One!
And we—

CROWD. Shake the Bag!

(*The violin re-emerges.*)

NEAERA. . . . Lento . . . accelerando . . . presto . . . calando . . .
morendo . . . .

(*The violin fades away; it is meant to have established an affaire
between Roland and Neaera.*)

STEWARD (*slyly*).
Well, sir? So the lady is still practising.
Golden days, sir, golden days.
At sea, sir, have you noticed

One doesn't notice time?
You probably feel you just came on board yesterday
And yet you got your sea-legs weeks ago, sir.

ROLAND. Sea-legs? Why, this trip has been so calm
I've never felt—

STEWARD. That's right, sir; never feel.
There's nothing in life but profit and pleasure.
Allegro assai—some people plump for pleasure
But I now fancy the profit—

(*Receiving a tip.*)

Ah thank you, sir, thank you.
The sea today in the sun, sir, looks like what shall I
say, sir?

ROLAND. The sea today? A dance of golden sovereigns.

NEAERA. The sea today is adagios of doves.

ROLAND. The sea today is gulls and dolphins.

NEAERA. The sea today is noughts and crosses.

OFFICER (*cutting in rapidly*).
And we—

CROWD. Shake the Bag!

NEAERA. The sea today, Roland, is crystal.

ROLAND. The sea today Neaera, is timeless.

NEAERA. The sea today is drums and fifes.

ROLAND. The sea today is broken bottles.

NEAERA. The sea today is snakes and ladders.

OFFICER (*as before*).
Especially snakes!

CROWD. Especially snakes!

NEAERA (*wheedling*).
Roland, what's that ring? I've never seen one like it.

ROLAND. There is no other ring like it.

NEAERA. A strange ring for a man . . .
My colour, you know—that red . . .
Why do you twitch your finger?

ROLAND. Because it burns.

NEAERA. It burns?

Like tingling ears perhaps? Someone is thinking of
you.

ROLAND (*startled—and suddenly depressed*).

What? . . . I hope not.

(*changing the subject*)

Come, darling, let's have a drink.

OFFICER. And we—

CROWD. Shake the Bag!

ROLAND. The sea today is drunken marble.

NEAERA. The sea today is silver stallions.

ROLAND. The sea today is—Tell me, steward:
Where's all this floating seaweed come from?

STEWARD. I imagine, sir—forgive me mentioning it—
That we are approaching land.

ROLAND. Land!

STEWARD. Yes, sir—but *you* won't be landing of course.
The best people never land, sir.

ROLAND. No? . . . (*to himself, fatalistically*) I suppose not.
(*Neaera's violin is heard again.*)

NEAERA (*to herself*).

. . . piu sonoro . . . con forza . . . accelerando . . .
crescendo . . . .

(*The orchestra is added for a final crashing chord and at once we hear the
hubbub of a crowd.*)

STENTOR. Anyone more for the shore? Anyone more for the
shore?

Line up there on the forward deck
All what wants to chance their neck!
Anyone more for the shore?

TICKET COLLECTOR.

This way: thank you—This way: thank you—
This way: thank you—This way: thank you.

STENTOR. Anyone more? Hurry up please!

But remember this: Once you're off

You can't come back not ever on board.

We leave at once. At once!

TICKET COLLECTOR.

This way: thank you—This way: thank you—This way: thank you—This way: thank you.

1ST PASSENGER (*cockney*).

Here, here, who're you shoving? What's the blinkin' hurry?

HIS WIFE. That's right.

1ST PASSENGER.

Some people seem very keen to land in the future.

Can't use their eyes—if you ask me!

HIS WIFE. That's right. Look at them vicious rocks.

1ST PASSENGER.

And that tumble-down shack what thinks it's a Customs House.

HIS WIFE. And them horrible mountains behind it.

2ND PASSENGER (*northern*).

You'd think this country was uninhabited.

TICKET COLLECTOR.

This way: thank you—This way: thank you— (*with finality*) This way: thank *you*!

(*wearily*) O.K., sir. That's the lot.

STENTOR. Gangway up! Gangway up!

Clear away there. Mind your heads!

NEAERA. What are you staring at, Roland?

Come away, chéri; the show's over.

There goes the gangway; we're moving out now.

What *are* you staring at, darling?

ROLAND (*to himself*).

Was that . . . was that . . . I couldn't see in the face of the sun but—

Steward, you've sharp eyes.

Did you see over there on the quay, sitting on a rusty bollard—

STEWARD. Hsh, sir, Neaera will hear you.

Yes, sir; a very nice piece.

She was looking at you, sir, too—staring in fact, one might say.

Seems to be staring still—but what's she doing now?

Climbing up on the bollard?

Good Lord, sir, that's bad form; she's making gestures.

SYLVIE (*distant cry*).

Roland! . . . Roland! . . .

ROLAND. Sylvie!

I knew it. Out of my way there!

STENTOR. Here, here, here! Stop him!

Man gone mad there! Don't let him jump!

(*General commotion.*)

NEAERA. Roland! Come back!

(*A loud splash from the orchestra.*)

STENTOR. Man overboard! Man overboard!

(*The crowd reacts excitedly.*)

STENTOR. Lifebuoy! Where's the lifebuoy?

VOICE. Garn! This here ship don't carry no lifebuoys.

Nor he won't need one. Look! He's climbing up on the quay.

(*The orchestral engines start up again.*)

OFFICER (*triumphantly*).

And we—

CROWD. Shake the Bag!

NEAERA (*now revealing her hardness*).

Well, James . . . That's that.

STEWARD. Yes, madam.

NEAERA. You can drop the madam now.

STEWARD. Yes, Neaera—my sweetie-pie.

NEAERA (*matter-of-fact*).

That's more like it, James, my great big he-man.

Come to my cabin now; we'll count the takings.

(*The fading engines take the liner to sea; Roland is left on the Shore, with Sylvie sobbing.*)

ROLAND (*dead-pan*).

There she goes now.

SYLVIE (*echoing him*).

There she goes now . . . .

(*then bursting out*)

Roland, you are a hypocrite!

ROLAND (*quietly—but ashamed*).

No, Sylvie; merely a sleep-walker.

Ugh! (*He shivers.*)

SYLVIE (*calm again*).

The sea must have been cold. Come, let's walk.

ROLAND. How did you get here, Sylvie?

SYLVIE (*a shade bitter*).

I followed you—but not on a luxury liner.

Mine was a cargo boat, its limit was seven knots.

ROLAND. And yet you got here first.

And now I suppose you regret it.

Are you going to leave me, Sylvie?

SYLVIE. How can I? We're marooned here.

This is a desolate land. (*With forced control*) I suggest we keep together.

ROLAND. You have the gift of forgiveness.

SYLVIE. I have the gift of common sense.

As you're bound to be seduced from your so-called Quest,

In future, Roland, leave the seducing to me.

Or can't I, perhaps, compete with your ladies of pleasure?

ROLAND. Pleasure? That was not pleasure.

SYLVIE. It was. But it was not happiness.

ROLAND. And *you* offer me happiness?

SYLVIE. You doubt that I have it to offer?

ROLAND. No, I don't doubt that. But my tutor always said
Happiness cannot be taken as a present.

SYLVIE. Forget your tutor. This is a foreign land
Where no one will interfere with us.

ROLAND. No one? No *man* perhaps.

SYLVIE. What do you mean by that?

ROLAND. Look round you, Sylvie. See the deserted port,
The ruined shacks, the slag-heaps covered with lichen
And behind it all the frown and fear of the forest.
This is the Dragon's demesne.

SYLVIE. Roland, how childish you are.

ROLAND. You think so? Look at this notice
That flaps here on the hoarding—
And this one and this one and this one.

SYLVIE (*reading*).

'Wanted for Murder' . . . 'Wanted for Murder' . . .
'Wanted'—

ROLAND. You're reading the words wrong. Not 'for', Sylvie;
'to!'

SYLVIE. 'Wanted to Murder'. You're right.
But what does it mean?

ROLAND. It means we are on a soil where murder pays.

SYLVIE. It pays in many places.

ROLAND. Yes, but here
The paymaster is the government—and pay-day
Is every day of the week.
The Dragon's doing, I tell you.

SYLVIE. Well, if it is, *you* cannot cure it.
At the best you can cure yourself—
(*tentatively*) And that only through love.

ROLAND. Love?

SYLVIE (*stronger*).

> Through me, Roland, through me.

> > (*pause*)

ROLAND (*quietly, as if solving a problem*).

> Yes, I think you're right.

> > (*Then with sudden decisiveness*)

> Sylvie, take this ring; I cannot wear it now,

> I have failed this ring—but this ring will not fail you.

SYLVIE. You mean . . . ?

ROLAND. Yes. Let me put it on your finger.

SYLVIE. Not yet, Roland. That must be done in a church.

ROLAND. And where can we find a church round here?

SYLVIE (*half abstracted*).

> What a strange colour. Like the blood of a child.

ROLAND. I repeat! Where can we find a church or a chapel here?

> (*The Tout pops up. He speaks in broken English.*)

TOUT. 'Scusa. Lady and gentleman want guide to chapel?

ROLAND. God! Where did this come from?

TOUT. Me? Me come from sewer.

> Me accredited guide—very good, very funny.

> Lady and gentleman see chapel today?

ROLAND. Where is this chapel of yours?

TOUT. Chapel not mine, chapel belong to God.

> Me take you there up this road, see.

> Me tell you history, very much history, cheap.

> (*A distant bell is heard, which continues as they speak.*)

TOUT. That chapel bell, tee-hee!

> Ting-a-ling for the wedding!

ROLAND. What wedding?

TOUT. Me not know No, sir, nobody know.

> Happy pair not come yet.

SYLVIE. Roland, this is a sign.

> Tell him to show us the way.

The Dark Tower

TOUT. Me show you the way sure.

Beautiful lady put best foot first.

Chapel up there in forest.

ROLAND. In the forest?

TOUT. Sure, boss. Chapel old.

Chapel in forest before forest grew.

But needs repairs now bad.

Haunted too—tee-hee!

ROLAND. Haunted!

TOUT. Sure, boss.

Plenty ghosts—tu-whit, tu-whoo.

Me need bonus for them ghosts.

ROLAND. You'll have your bonus. Only get us there quick.

Sylvie, we will exorcise these ghosts.

You know how, my dearest?

SYLVIE (*heart-felt*).

I know how.

(*The bell continues but is gradually submerged by orchestral chapel music. The latter swells to a definite close, leaving Roland and Sylvie in the Haunted Chapel. The voices echo in the emptiness.*)

PRIEST (*old and tired but kindly*).

You have the ring? Good.

Before I complete this ceremony making you man and wife

I must deliver a warning.

The original sin is doubt.

And in these days of contempt for the individual

It is also the topical sin.

So if either of you has doubts of the holiness of marriage

Or if either of you has doubts of the other

And can conceive a time when he or she

Will think again and wish this thing undone,

Now is your time to speak.

(*pause*)

Good. So you have no doubts. There is one other
    formality.

Although there is no congregation present,

Although apart from ourselves and a few sparrows
    and field-mice

This chapel is now empty, I must still put the
    question:

If anyone here know just cause or impediment—

(*He is interrupted by voices with a strange acoustic.*)

BLIND PETER'S VOICE.

    I do!

GAVIN'S VOICE.

    I do!

FATHER'S VOICE.

    I do!

BLIND PETER'S VOICE.

    This young man who's come to you to get married
    Promised me when he left, a week before I died,
    As he would avenge my blindness and bring it about
    How no one should go the way I went in future.
    Well, has he done it? No, and he'll never do it—
    Not if you splice him up to that poor simple girl
    Who only dreams how he and she will be happy.

GAVIN'S VOICE.

    No, Roland, my brother; Blind Peter is right.
    Forget your dreams of a home. You can never be
      happy
    If you forsake the Quest. And if you could—
    Happiness is not all. You must go on—
    Turn your back on this chapel, go on through the
      forest,
    Alone, always alone, and then across the desert,
    And at the other end of that desert—

The Dark Tower

FATHER'S VOICE (*very deep*).

> You will find what I found, Roland.

ROLAND. You?

FATHER'S VOICE.

> You should know my voice though you never heard it.
>
> Though you had not seen me, you knew my portrait.

ROLAND. My father?

FATHER'S VOICE.

> I am still waiting to be your father.
>
> While you malinger, you are no son of mine.

ROLAND (*shattered*).

> Sylvie . . . .

SYLVIE. I know what you want . . . Your ring.

> (*She tries to retain self-control in making her renunciation.*)
>
> There . . . Back on your finger.
>
> Look how it glows in this darkness.

ROLAND (*bitterly*).

> Glows? It will burn me up.

SYLVIE. Roland, before we part—

PRIEST. This chapel is now closed. I am sorry.

> Goodbye, my daughter; your way lies back,
>
> Back by the road you came over the hopeless sea,
>
> Back to your little house and your apple orchard
>
> And there must you marry one of your own kind
>
> And spray the trees in spring and raise the ladders in autumn
>
> And spread the shining crop on the spare-room floor and—

ROLAND. Sylvie, before we part—

PRIEST. This chapel is now closed. I am sorry.

> Goodbye, my son; your way lies forward,
>
> Forward through the gibbering guile of the forest,
>
> Forward through the silent doubt of the desert.
>
> And here let me warn you: if in the forest

The Dark Tower

You hear any voices call from the trees,
Pay no attention, Roland, pay no attention . . . .

(His voice fades as forest music grows up; out of its tangle come the voices of the Birds, harsh and mechanical, speaking in a heavily stressed sing-song rhythm.)

PARROT. Pretty Polly! Pretty Polly!
Who's this coming now?

RAVEN. Caw-caw! Caw-caw!
Who's a-walkin' in *my* forest?

PARROT. Pretty Polly! The leaves have fallen.

RAVEN. Caw-caw! He's walking late.

PARROT. Pretty Polly! He's looking pale.

RAVEN. Caw-caw! His bones will be paler.

PARROT. Pretty Polly! Here he comes.

RAVEN. Caw-caw! Greet him!

PARROT *(sneeringly)*.
Where are you going, Roland, so fast?

RAVEN. Roland, running away from your past?

BOTH. You can't do *that*! You can't do *that*!

PARROT. Still on the road? Still on the Quest?

RAVEN. None achieve it but the best.

BOTH. You're not the sort. You're not the sort.

PARROT. Why not stop, my dear young man?

RAVEN. Let heroes die as heroes can.

BOTH. *You* must *live*! *You* must *live*!

(The forest music swells up as Roland passes.)

PARROT. Pretty Polly! He's passed us by.

RAVEN. Caw-caw! The devil take him.

PARROT. Pretty Polly! The devil will.

(The forest music gives place to desert music and Roland is heard soliloquising.)

ROLAND *(very tired)*.
Oh this desert!
The forest was bad enough but this beats all.

The Dark Tower

When my tutor described it to me, it sounded strange
But now I am here, with the grit of it filling my shoes,
I find that the worst thing about it is this:
The desert is something familiar.
And with no end—no end.

(The music ends. A mechanical voice creeps in.)

CLOCK VOICE.

Tick Tock, Tick Tock,
Sand and grit, bones and waste,
A million hours—all the same,
A million minutes—each an hour,
And nothing stops for nothing starts
But the hands move, the dead hands move,
The desert is the only clock—
Tick Tock, Tick Tock,
Tick Tock, Tick Tock . . . .

*(The Clock Voice recedes but can just be heard ticking as Roland speaks,
with the Desert registering again musically.)*

ROLAND. Flat—No shape—No colour—Only here and there
A mirage of the past—something I've met before—
Figures arising from dust, repeating themselves,
Telling me things that I have no wish to remember.
Mirage . . . mirage . . . mirage . . . .

(The music ends and the Clock comes near again.)

CLOCK VOICE.

Tick Tock, Tick Tock,
Tick Tock, Tick Tock . . . .

(continuing in the background as the first mirage is heard.)

SOAK. A pretty boy—but I've given him no more lines.
He'd never guess what happens in my dream.
Look—a pull on the wire, his feet move forward.
Left Right, Left Right . . . .

*(He synchronises with the Clock Voice as it comes again into the
foreground.)*

57

CLOCK VOICE.⎫ Tick Tock etc.
SOAK.⎭ Left Right etc.

(*They withdraw to the background as the second mirage appears.*)

STEWARD. Golden days, sir, golden days.
In the desert, sir, have you noticed
One doesn't notice time?
But I thought so the moment I saw you:
You don't know where you're going.
Golden days, golden days . . . .

(*He synchronises with the Clock Voice and Soak—the same procedure.*)

CLOCK VOICE.⎫ Tick Tock, etc.
SOAK.⎬ Left Right, etc.
STEWARD.⎭ Golden days, etc.

NEAERA. . . . . adagio . . . rallentando . . .
This dossier includes your future—
You don't come out of it well.
But kiss me, Roland, kiss me.
Kiss me, kiss me . . . .

(*synchronises*)

CLOCK VOICE.⎫ Tick Tock, etc.
SOAK.⎪ Left Right, etc.
STEWARD.⎬ Golden days, etc.
NEAERA.⎭ Kiss me, etc.

SYLVIE. But why must you go so quickly?
Now that the sun's come out.
You, Roland—you're no knight errant.
Your love for me will triumph, you'll come back,
Then you and I, you and I . . . .

(*synchronises*)

CLOCK VOICE.⎫ Tick Tock, etc.
SOAK.⎪ Left Right, etc.
STEWARD.⎬ Golden days, etc.
NEAERA.⎪ Kiss me, etc.
SYLVIE.⎭ You and I, etc.

The Dark Tower

(The five voices swell in the foreground, driving as it were at the camera,
till Roland can bear it no longer.)

ROLAND *(screaming)*.

NO!

(The voices break off as if cut with a knife.)

ROLAND. Shapes of dust and fancy! Unreal voices!

But where is the voice that launched me on my
road?

Where is the shape the first that I remember?

Why doesn't *she* appear—even in fancy?

It is the least she could—Mother, where are you?

Yes, you; I'm calling you—my mother who sent me
forth—

It was all your doing. But for you

I who had no beliefs of my own,

I who had no will of my own,

Should not be here today pursuing

A dark tower that is only dark

Because it does not exist. And Mother!

It is only your will that drives me still

As signified in the blood-red stone

I wear on my finger under my glove

That burns me like a living weal.

(suddenly puzzled)

. . . Burns me? . . . Burns me? . . . It always has—

But have I gone numb? I can feel nothing.

Off with this glove! I *can't* believe that—

(A chord from the orchestra.)

ROLAND. The ring! The ring!

The colour is gone; the blood has gone out of it.

But that must mean . . . that means . . . .

MOTHER'S VOICE *(in a different acoustic, whispering)*.

It means, my son, that I want you back.

ROLAND. And the Quest then?

59

MOTHER. Lapses.

> On my deathbed I have changed my mind;
> I am bearing now a child of stone.
>
> *He* can go on the Quest. But you, Roland—come back!

(*A pause while Roland takes in the implications.*)

ROLAND. The ring . . . is always right.

> Recall! Reprieve! A thousand years of sunshine!
> And the apples will be in bloom round Sylvie's house.
> Was that my mother's voice? Look at the ring.
> It is as pale as death, there is no more breach of duty,
> Her will is not behind me. Breach of duty?
> If she is dying, *there* is the breach of duty—
> Not to be there. Mother, you sent me out
> And I went out. Now that you call me back
> I will come back! The desert take this ring—
> It serves no further purpose!

(*An orchestral clink as he throws away the ring.*)

ROLAND (*startled*).

> What was that?
> It must have struck something hard. That's the first
> Sound I've heard in the desert. Where did I throw
> that ring?
> A stone? But a carved stone! Looks like a milestone.
> As if the desert had any use for milestones!

(*with a hysterical half-laugh*)

> How many miles to Babylon? Let's see now;
> These letters are choked with sand, 'To Those . . .
> To Those . . .'

(*He deciphers the inscription, reading it aloud slowly.*)

> 'To Those Who Did Not Go Back—
> Whose Bones being Nowhere, their signature is for
> All Men—
> Who went to their Death of their Own Free Will
> Bequeathing Free Will to Others.'

The Dark Tower

(The Bird Voices cut in, in a different acoustic, jeering.)

PARROT. Pretty Polly! A tall story!

RAVEN. Caw-caw! And not so new!

PARROT. Pretty Polly! Unknown warriors!

RAVEN. Caw-caw! Nobody cares!

PARROT. 'Who went to their death!'—Pretty Polly!

RAVEN. 'Of their own free will!'—Caw-caw!

ROLAND. Of their own free will? It wasn't like that with me.
It was my mother pushed me to this point
And now she pulls me back. Let's see this ring —
Where's it fallen? Hm. Yes, there's no mistake,
Red no longer: my mother wants me back
And indeed it is high time; this desert has no end
Nor even any contour, the blank horizon
Retreats and yet retreats; without either rise or fall
Repeats, retreats, defeats; there is no sign of a
 tower—
You could see a tower for miles; there is not even a
 knoll,
Flatness is all—and nothing. Own free will?
(He has been speaking quietly but now bursts out.)
As if I Roland had ever . . . . Tutors, trumpeters,
 women,
Old soaks and crooked stewards, everyone I have met
Has played his music on me. Own free will!
Three words not one of which I understand!
All right, Mother dear, I'm coming.
　　　　　　(Pause.)
Now . . . Where are my footsteps? Better follow
 them back.
Back to the forest and through it and so to the shore
 of the sea.
Are these my footsteps? But how small they look!
Well, you're a small man, Roland—Better admit it—

You'll be still smaller now . . . But are these my
    footsteps?
They are so near together—and I thought
I was walking with great strides! O Roland, Roland,
You thought yourself a hero—and you walked
With little steps like that! Now you must watch
These niggling foot-prints all your return journey
To underline your shame. What's shame to me
Who never had free will? . . . 'their own free will
Bequeathing free will to others.' Others indeed!
I begin to think my drunken friend was right
In his subjective tavern; there are no others
Apart from the projections of my mind
And, once that mind is empty, man's a desert.

(*losing his temper*)

    Others! Who are these others? Where can I find 'em?

CHILD'S VOICE (*out of the blue*).

    Nowhere, Roland. Nowhere.

ROLAND. There! What did I say? There *are* no—

CHILD'S VOICE.

    You will never find us if you go forward—
    For you will be dead before we are born.
    You will never find us if you go back—
    For you will have killed us in the womb.

ROLAND. What! So I'm an infanticide now?

CHILD'S VOICE.

    Not yet. But if you go back . . .

ROLAND. Who said I was going back?

CHILD'S VOICE.

    I thought you had made up your mind.

ROLAND. I never make up my mind!
    Didn't I say that my mother—Look, I'll leave it to
      chance;
    Chance is as good an arbiter as any.

The Dark Tower

Watch me, you unborn children. See this tiny cactus?
I will strip it leaf by leaf—let that decide—
This Year, Next Year, Eena-Meena—*you* know the
game, you unborn children.
Now.

(He counts in regular time, but with growing tension, as he picks off the leaves.)

Forward—back; forward—back; forward—back—
forward;
Back—forward; back—forward; back—forward—
back;
Forward—back; forward—back; forward—back—
forward;
Back—forward; back—forward; back—forward—
BACK.
There! The voice of chance. The oracle of the cactus.
Back! Back! That's what the cactus says.
But *I'm* . . .

(He holds the suspense, then with decision.)

. . . going forward, children!
Did you think that I'd let a cactus dictate to me?
Mother, don't pull on the string; you must die alone.
Forgive me, dear, but—I tell you I'm going forward.
Forward, Roland . . . into the empty desert,
Where all is flat and colourless and silent.

(He pauses; the orchestra creeps in with a heart-beat rhythm.)

Silent? . . . Then what's this?
Something new! A *sound*! But a sound of what?
Don't say that it's my heart! Why, Roland you poor
fool,
Who would think you had one? You must be afraid;
It is fear reveals the heart.

(Heart-beat louder.)

ROLAND. Aha, you piece of clockwork—

63

Trying to have your little say while you can!

Before your wheels run down here in the empty desert.

(*Sudden chord; the heart-beat continues.*)

Empty? . . . Where have those mountains come from?

Closing round in a ring. Hump-backed horrors

That want to be in at the death. And where's the horizon?

A moment ago this was level. What's the game?

A confidence trick? A trap! I am cooped in.

A circle of ugly cliffs—a lobster-pot of rock!

Silence, my stupid heart! This looks like . . . looks like what?

This looks like the great circus in Ancient Rome,

Only there is no audience—and no lions.

(*suddenly noticing*)

No audience?

(*Chord; heart-beat behind—and steadily increasing.*)

No audience! Why, that's Gavin on top of that peak!

And Michael and Denis and Henry and Roger and John!

And men that I've never seen—in outlandish clothes,

Some of them even in armour. And there's Blind Peter—

With sight in his eyes, for he's pointing—

And my father too—I remember him from the album—

And my tutor—he must be dead—looking graver than ever

And—well to the front of course—my dear old Sergeant-Trumpeter.

(*Figure in the music; the succeeding voices, other than Roland's own, sound as if coming from somewhere far-off and above.*)

SERGEANT-TRUMPETER.

Roland! Hold the note at the end.

GAVIN. Be ready, old boy. This is it!

BLIND PETER.

      Strike a good blow to avenge Blind Peter.

FATHER. Your heritage, my son. You were born to fight and—

ROLAND. Fight? Fight whom? This circus has no lions.

TUTOR. No lions, Roland? Have you forgotten your lessons?
      I never mentioned lions; it was a dragon—
      And only that for lack of a better name.

ROLAND. Yes, yes, dragon of course—but you told me, my
      good tutor,
      The Dragon would not appear until I came to the
      Tower
      And until I had blown my blast—Well, there is no
      tower!

GAVIN. That fooled *me*, Roland my brother.

FATHER. Look over there, Roland my son.

ROLAND. Where? . . . Oh *that* little thing?
      Like a wart coming out of the ground!

FATHER. It's growing, Roland, it's growing.

TUTOR. You should recognise it from my lectures.

BLIND PETER.

      That's the joker all right.

              (*Figure in the music.*)

GAVIN. The tower! The Dark Tower!

SERGEANT-TRUMPETER.

      Quick now, my lad. Unsling your trumpet.

ROLAND. But—

FATHER. It's growing, my son; waste no time.

ROLAND. It's growing; yes, it's growing.

CHILD'S VOICE.

      Growing! Ooh! Look at it.

      Strike a good blow for us unborn children.

MOTHER (*closer than the rest*).

      And strike a blow for all dead mothers.

GAVIN. Jump to it, Roland.

FATHER. Waste no time.

SERGEANT-TRUMPETER.

Remember that challenge call.

Blow it the way I taught you.

ROLAND (*beginning quiet but resolute and building*).

Yes, dear friends, I will blow it the way you taught
me.

I Roland, the black sheep, the unbeliever—

Who never did anything of his own free will—

Will do this now to bequeath free will to others.

(*full out*) Ahoy there, tower, Dark Tower, you're getting big,

Your shadow is cold upon me. What of that?

And you, you Dragon or whatever you are

Who make men beasts, come out—here is a man;

Come out and do your worst.

(*The heart-beat, having reached its crescendo, ends clean.*)

ROLAND (*restrained, in the sudden silence*).

Wrist be steady

As I raise the trumpet so—now fill my lungs—

(*The Challenge Call rings out; the Sergeant-Trumpeter speaks as the last
long note is reached.*)

SERGEANT-TRUMPETER.

Good lad, Roland. Hold that note at the end.

(*The trumpet holds it, enriched and endorsed by the orchestra. They come
to a full close and that is* THE END.)